Living Life with LIFE

Living Life with LIFE

Beverley Lower Estes

AuthorHouse™
1663 Liberty Drive
Bloomington, IN 47403
www.authorhouse.com
Phone: 1-800-839-8640

© 2012 by Beverley Lower Estes. All rights reserved.

No part of this book may be reproduced, stored in a retrieval system, or transmitted by any means without the written permission of the author.

Published by AuthorHouse   07/10/2012

ISBN: 978-1-4772-0141-1 (sc)
ISBN: 978-1-4772-0142-8 (hc)
ISBN: 978-1-4772-0140-4 (e)

Library of Congress Control Number: 2012908469

Any people depicted in stock imagery provided by Thinkstock are models, and such images are being used for illustrative purposes only.
Certain stock imagery © Thinkstock.

This book is printed on acid-free paper.

Because of the dynamic nature of the Internet, any web addresses or links contained in this book may have changed since publication and may no longer be valid. The views expressed in this work are solely those of the author and do not necessarily reflect the views of the publisher, and the publisher hereby disclaims any responsibility for them.

Dedicated to the Creator

This book is my life with LIFE, LOVE, GRACE, FAITHFULNESS, THE SAVIOR and the Way of LIFE.

HE is faithful to all who want HIM. HE wants to help all see that they need Him.

Thank you Lord for who YOU are and all YOU have done and continue to do for YOUR world and Men and Women.

Lord my asking of YOU is that now help us take the way of the King HIMSELF-the mind of Christ, the emotions of Christ, the will of Christ, the heart of Christ, the Love of Christ. All of HIM into ourselves for YOUR glory and our good.

None of our flesh. Help us to be in complete and total union with who YOU are.

A thank you for our daughter Nicci who was named by her dad, after God. The gift I see from YOU in her is treating others tenderly as a nurse most of all.

A thank you for our oldest son Derek for the gifts that I see strongest in him. Consideration for others.

A thank you for Link our youngest son and for the gift I see most in him, is wanting to keep his word to others.

YOU LORD, have used them greatly to teach me YOUR ways, and I thank them for allowing me to make mistakes and YOU taught me through them.

A thank you for Stan, husband and father, for being the one YOU chose for us as he had to be the kind of husband and father that did not try to run the life of anyone else. (That is sin) He allowed us to live life for YOU. That took me to Israel and then Africa because he was willing. Thank you for that gift to him and that he was able to share it with all of us.

Thank you for my extended family. Thank you for who they are, for living their lives so I could see how to live mine. The Lower's, the Watson's, the Ratcliff's, the Wright's, the James', the Pennington's, and other extended family.

Special Thanks

I would like to thank my classmates from Sublette for the impact that you had on my life. You helped make me who I am today. Keith Armentrout, Jim Bailey, Gladys Bale, James Brown, Duane Caldwell, Howard Coffman, Jack Connor, Shirley Eldridge, Rita Knoettgen, Herbert Livingston, Verna Makerson, Bob Martin, Bill McGehee, Ann Miller, Frances Miller, John Phipps, Ralph Schmidt, Bonita Smith, and Alice Talley

Special Recognition

Shanna Larson Lindberg; a special recognition for typing the script and helping to correct the book for errors. I want to thank her for who she is and a true gift from God. A great personality and grace abounds in you/her, your greatest gift from God.

We have heard the saying, "It is the best of times and it is the worst of times." I was soon to learn, as a child, that is the way it is on this earth Living Life with "LIFE," Jesus.

It would seem that when I was born it was the worst of times. Our little house had no indoor plumbing, no running water, no electricity, no refrigerator and no phone. At some point, we got a car. We had to drive eight miles to buy food.

All six of us were born at home in this house. I do not know who helped my mom, except her mom, my grandmother, Lila. Grandma had come out to help my mom until she gained her strength back from having me. She was already cooking for a one-year-old and a four-year-old son, in addition to hired men.

My Grandmother took me to town to care for me until my mom was stronger. She did not return with me when my mother wanted her to. Mother finally went to town to get me. My aunt Sarah, mom's youngest sister, said I was crying, my mom was crying and Grandma was crying. Finally, Sarah said to her mother, give her to Lena as it is her child.

You would think that I would have felt a great deal of love, because both loved me, but it worked just the reverse. Not knowing this until I grew up I always felt like I did not belong anywhere. By sharing this with my Aunt at my mom's 80th birthday, she told me the previous story.

When Aunt Sarah's husband died we were asked to share something about Uncle Maurice that showed who he was with the Lord. Mom was at the funeral, I started sharing. My mom recognized my voice, looked at me, and said, "You are mine, not theirs." I said that is right mom, I am yours. I realized it had also affected her. To this day I do not feel like I belong no matter where I am except one place.

I found that place when I was five years old. I heard my grandmother tell Jack, my oldest brother, about Jesus. My second brother, Stuart, was listening too. I was thinking I wanted Jesus in the worst way when Stuart said, "Grandma, can I have HIM too?" "No you are too young to understand," she said. Therefore, I thought, Stuart is just six, so if he is too young then she will tell me the same thing.

I just kept quiet but was determined in my heart to have Jesus, no matter what. No one was going to keep HIM from me. I really think the Lord used this feeling of never belonging, as "He" was a place I could and would belong.

The next Sunday all three of us went forward and accepted Christ as our personal Savior. Oh yes, the pastor, Grandma's brother, tried to talk Stuart and I out of it as we were too young. Neither one of us budged.

It was now time in my life that I was to start learning from just Living Life with "LIFE." It was going to happen with my relationship with the Lord and the HOLY SPIRIT.

After I was baptized my Grandmother, Mattie, came to me and said, "Now the HOLY SPIRIT will come to you." All this did was create many questions. Will I see HIM? Will it be a man or a woman? What will he or she want or do? This started a pattern for me that I have to this day. If I don't know, I say nothing to people, put it in the back of my mind and wait on the Lord. He will do His work even if I don't know where, what, when, how or who.

It was not until years later that one day, I read an article in Kenneth Copeland's magazine, written by his wife Gloria. She was telling of her struggle of the indwelling of the HOLY SPIRIT until someone challenged her to read Matthew, Mark, Luke and John three times through in one month. She did and she said she knew who the HOLY SPIRIT was. I took the challenge too and I added Acts, being the book that talks most about the HOLY SPIRIT. By the end of the month, I knew I wanted the HOLY SPIRIT indwelling. I knew it was something God would give me. Therefore, I got on my knees and asked for it.

Nothing happened. I did that the second night, asking the Lord for the indwelling. Nothing, and I got the distinct feeling God was saying you are not sure you really desired it. The third night I was in the mode you can't keep her from me. I received and began speaking in tongues and praising God. My level of thankfulness had gone off the charts. I learned that The HOLY SPIRIT brings peace, joy and thankfulness to a degree I never dreamed was possible. I then knew what God was saying in the scripture about the men with the HOLY SPIRIT, that others thought them drunk. Boldness was another thing I noticed I was telling everyone who came to my preschool all about Jesus, and the joy of knowing He is real.

I began to see that if I was not taught by my relationship with "LIFE," I would not learn it from man's way of knowing. Too often, it is from their flesh. Besides when "LIFE" teaches me I do not forget.

I need to back up now and tell about some of those experiences of the HOLY SPIRIT doing the teaching. Yes, I had the HOLY SPIRIT at Baptism, but it was as if God turned up the heat. The HOLY SPIRIT we get at Baptism is like a pilot light on a stove, but the indwelling is like God turning up the heat to get the job done.

Years later, HE taught me through scripture, that everything has spirit. So, the HOLY SPIRIT is in everything. The scriptures said, SPIRIT is fire, cloud, male, female, fruits, animals, every living thing has SPIRIT.

Back to being five and being very determined to be all Jesus wanted me to be. I wanted so desperately to go to summer camp to study God's word. There was an age limit as kids got home sick if they went too young. I knew I would not as I did not belong anywhere except to Jesus.

It turned out that I did get to go one year earlier than the set age. I look back on that and I really think because both of my brothers were there the adults thought that I'd be okay with two big brothers. I hardly saw them at camp. Oh, yes I did from a distance when they were playing games with their team across the field. We did not sit at the same tables and were not on the same teams so the only time I saw them was if we played against each other.

Camp was such a high, as I do not remember anyone fighting, getting mad at each other or talking about anyone as gossip. When I got home, it was like back to earth and the real world. It was a letdown, but God used this as wisdom learned for later use to understand what others are feeling and why they act out.

When I was eight or nine at camp, we were always to go out as soon as we got up and spend 15 minutes with the Lord. This day I was disillusioned and asked the Lord "Is this all there is to this walk with you?"

At that moment, it was if something warm was being poured upon my head and I felt the warmth flow downward. That was all I needed, as I knew there was more, even if I did not know what God did in that moment.

Then when I was nine, I was playing with my four best friends on the playground, Gladys, Karen, Verna and Pauline. They all took off and I did not have the desire to go. I was just standing by the bar swing daydreaming. I suddenly wondered if I missed the bell from sounding, as it seemed very quiet. I looked up, turned around and saw no students and the school grounds were as quiet as they could be.

I thought well I'm in trouble so I'll just be in trouble, as I was not ready to go yet. Then the Lord spoke to me. "You are going to have something to do with parentless children." Then the bell rang and there were all the students and the noise. I just wondered how God did that.

I began to realize that to have the HOLY SPIRIT teach me and train me in the way I should go was like going on a treasure hunt. He never gives all the information as he wanted me to continue seeking and looking to HIM. I was going to learn this the hard way. As a child when parents ask you to do something you go and do it. So, that is what I started doing. I started planning that I would be a missionary as that was the only place I had ever heard of where children had no parents and by the time I graduated I was excited to know of a place in Oklahoma City that trained nurses for missions.

As I was sharing my excitement with my mother she said, "I will not pay for it." "If I can find a job and pay for it myself?" She said "Yes!" I called Oklahoma City and found a job in a crippled children's home where I could go to work as soon as I could get there.

I told mother I had a job and they needed Gladys, my best friend, and myself. My mother said, "You still are not going." I asked why because earlier she had said yes. "Because the school is not an accredited school, you could not find a job anywhere in the United States unless it is accredited.

I cried for three days and was bitter towards my mother. It never occurred to me to disobey her and go anyway. I decided to go to Fort Hays University. My home economics teacher picked Gladys and I up and took us to the drug store where we were headed. As we rode she asked Gladys what she was going to do and she said go to Fort Hays to college.

Then she asked me what my plans were and I said the same as Gladys. The teacher said, "I don't know why you are going. You'll never make it." That infuriated me and I began to set my will and remember thinking, well you old witch I'll show you.

God needed me to set my will to do this as I did not know just how hard I was going to have to work. I did not know that I had dyslexia and was going deaf. By the time I was a senior my French teacher asked me to have my ears checked as she was convinced I was deaf or almost deaf. I remember thinking, oh yea just another reason to get me to give up. I was checked and I had 10 percent in one ear and 20 percent in the other, which is considered legally deaf. I then realized how God, through being deaf had placed determination in me.

I was very excited as I began to see God working. He had shown me that what I had been doing from the sixth grade until now was separation from God, and it would cause me trouble in the future. God showed that if HE had not corrected me I would have been lost to HIM. The rest of my years were setting my will and asking the Lord, so I thought. I would not get married as I never felt like I belonged anywhere.

Setting My Will

I was at my Grandma Mattie's house and she was crying about something her neighbor did that was hurtful to her. Her daughter, Ione, was there and she was going over to the neighbor's house to let her have it. Grandma Mattie stopped crying right then and said, "No you won't as it is bad enough that she hurt me and it would be worse if we gave back evil for evil." Once again, I learned about life by living "LIFE."

That day I also set my will not to cry like Grandmother as it caused others to want to defend and return evil for evil. To this day, it is very hard for me to cry except because of compassion toward God. God's compassion can cause tears, but later I learned tears are our greatest prayers and God catches every one. Now I would rather cry more.

The One Room School House

Another traumatic experience was in the third grade. We had a new teacher. She was young and not much taller than my older brother Jack, who was in sixth grade. The teacher had asked me to go to the board and write my five times tables. I said "I don't know what that is," and she told me that I did too, and to go to the board and write them. I went and just stood there. I turned around, for what I did not know. My brother Stuart was holding up his big tablet with the number five filling the page so I could see it.

I wrote five on the board and the teacher said, "See you little liar, you do know them." Now I was really in trouble, as I did not know what was next. Stuart put 10 on the page as big as he could and held it up for me, but the teacher caught him. She grabbed the ruler to crack the backs of his hands, but he jumped up and started running. She could not catch him, he was a fast one, so she got the broom as that would reach farther and she was closing in on him.

The old country school had the old desks that were all one unit. Stuart yelled put up your seats, and we did. He then slid under the desks to the other side of the room. By now, I was standing on top of my desk yelling for Stuart to run, slide, dodge or whatever he needed to do. It was a three-ring circus. It's strange that I do not remember how it ended. Maybe we went to recess.

Another day the teacher was giving me my spelling words. She watched how I spelled each one. About the third one, I misspelled it and she slapped me in the face and said spell it right. Well that kept me from even thinking let alone spelling the word right. My brother Jack sat right across from me and he was reading and was able to concentrate completely. He did not even know that she had slapped me. She turned to Jack and asked him for his belt.

He heard her but he was still concentrating on what he was reading. She said give me your belt, as she was going to use it on me. He started unbuckling his belt while still reading. I wanted to scream at him not to do what he was doing. Just before he pulled it completely out of his jeans loops, he came out of his concentration, "What do you want with my belt?"

She said just give it to me and he said no. Jack was my hero at that moment. The teacher slapped him in the face and sent his glasses flying across the room to the front. Things got deadly quiet and Jack walked up to the front and got his glasses.

He looked them over and they were not damaged. He walked back to his seat and said, "If you would have broken them, then you would be in big trouble." She was greatly shaken and that ended the push and shove incident. I do not remember if I finished my spelling test.

We kept telling our parents about all this but that was in 1947 when the rule was, you get into trouble at school and you will get it twice as severe when you get home. As I look back, I am sure it seemed too shocking for parents to take seriously.

One day my brother Stuart asked to go to the outhouse. The teacher refused to let him go, not knowing he had diarrhea. Consequently, he had an accident and she had to call our mother to come get him.

We finally had enough of her poor treatment towards us and we decided to take matters into our own hands. My dad had just gotten one of the new nylon ropes that were advertized as indestructible. We brought it to school and tied ourselves and all the other students into the coal and horse barn. This rope would keep us safe. The teacher rang the bell and no one came.

She came looking for us and found us. She could not get in and we were not about to come out as we all knew what she was capable of doing. She got into her car and left. We were jumping up and down with glee, thinking we had won and gotten rid of her. Then the car came back into the schoolyard and as she was walking toward us, we saw she had a butcher knife.

She was going to kill us all. In all of the excitement, no one thought anything, except get out. There was only one way out besides the door, a small window, with no glass, high up under the peak of the roof. The bigger kids could jump and grab the edge and squeeze through the window.

They were escaping while she cut dad's nylon rope. She was almost through when Stuart said, "I'll help you up." I still could not reach the window edge. So I said, "Stuart I've seen you run up a wall, so run up the wall and get out." He did and had just caught the bottom edge when the teacher got through. She picked up an old two by four board and hit him hard across the back and he dropped, as a fly would, hit by a fly swatter.

I thought she had killed him. She froze and was contemplating her next move. He just had his wind knocked out. When he got up she started after us and Stuart said you go one way around her and I'll go the other. We did and by the time she made up her mind which one of us to catch we were out the door and running with all we had in us towards home.

When we reached home, a mile and a half later, we were still as white as fresh Cloroxed sheets. Mom and dad finally believed us. We did not have to go to school the next day. I was riding a tricycle on our long wooden floor porch when the teacher came upon the porch to talk to mom.

She did not seem to have any hold of me and I felt no bitterness towards her. But, as she talked to mom she was trying to convince her that this was my fault and to me that spelled pitting my mom against me. Then anger rose up like a violent ocean wave. I had been at the far end of the porch and I starting riding towards her full speed and I was going to take her out. My mom opened the screen door between the teacher and myself and just said to me, "No."

Somehow, I got her point that she knew what the teacher was doing and all was well. I was immediately at peace and felt no hate or resentment towards her. They hired a new teacher and he had a party each month to show us school could be fun. My favorite memory is when we made taffy and pulled the candy and then got to eat it.

The next year we all went to town school, by school bus. It was the best of times and it was the worst of times as Dad had finished our new house and we were able to move in before going to town school.

I am still amazed at how I had no hate for the teacher. I think the overriding principle is how my brothers and family defended me and supported me. In having family support, I did not need to hate anyone. "Life" was there to surround me in my family. I also found things to be thankful. My twin sisters, Charlotte and Charon, had not started school yet nor my youngest brother Guy. I can't fathom how mistreatment like that would have affected them, besides they did not know Jesus yet. Without realizing it, HE is all I needed. He provided all I had need of and that was love through others.

Town School

When I walked into my fourth grade classroom I did not know where to sit, I did not want to be where the teacher could see me. After I chose the last seat in the back row so that everyone was in my sight the Lord said, "Watch what others do." One day I was going to the front and a boy was coming to the back. I had a notebook in my hands and as we got closer, I knew he was planning something. Sure enough, he tried to kiss me, only I quickly put the notebook in front of my face and he kissed the notebook.

That whole year when a student would do something funny, mean or smart-alecky, the Lord would ask me, "Why did they do that?" For the most part, I did not know. It was the beginning of learning how to have a relationship with HIM. In time, I would ask HIM why.

It always had to do with the heart, hurt and anger. Much later in life I learned, under all anger is fear. I then realized why God told us to fear not. That can stop or detour us unless we have a relationship with HIM. I began to realize God never got mad at me, or called me stupid when we talked. I could ask HIM anything and not be slapped, put down or called a liar.

I began to fall in love with HIM and in time, because he first loved me, I could love others that same way. As I saw how Jesus treated me in our conversations, I did not want to have relationships with others that much. People just did not accept me like my Father God did. HE never put me down, HE never scolded me, HE never shamed me or HE never said, "Before I was so rudely interrupted," like Jesus told Mack in the book <u>The Shack</u>, when others need to do any of that it is because one is still under the law.

Responsibilities and expectations are the basis of guilt, shame and judgment. I was already learning what it is like not to live up to someone's expectations. Expectation says you did not flush the toilet, you did not sweep the floor or wash the clothes.

I began to see in the "word" Jesus. HE always came asking, seeking, knocking to find even though HE already knew. But, HE was here to show us "The Way." Jesus was THE WAY and in my relationship with HIM. I started noticing what HE said and what HE did, just like HE said in HIS word, "I only say what I hear MY Father saying and I only do what I see my Father doing."

So must I be the same in a relationship with HIM to know who He is? Since I have so much of the word in me I had to learn the hard way a lot of the time. As I went through grade school, we got electric lines to our farm and telephone lines. Even though it was what we called "Crank and holler," it was a way to call a doctor or the pastor.

Dad had a rule of only three minutes per call as the phone was for business. Sometimes I liked that as I did not have to talk very long with others and did not have much to say to them, but I did think it fun to listen in on our party line of four.

Just like now, people would get on and gossip. Even in doing that, the Lord taught me it was out of fear. It always seemed like anger but in time I saw it was what they feared. I saw I was no different with anger. I do not remember being angry much, but did one day. Only it turned around.

Running Away

I knew I feared I was not wanted, needed or even cared about. I decided to run away to prove my point. I went as far as the hired man's bunkhouse and got tired of just sitting and waiting for the day to end. I fell asleep and when I woke up it was almost sun down. I was then worried that I was in trouble. I went to the house and everyone proved my point. No one missed me. Mom just said wash up for supper.

I had a decision to make as to how to handle this information. I decided it was a good thing and I could spend more time with the Lord and no one would miss me. I would leave the house at night and spend time with the Lord in the dark, peace and quiet of nature.

These were the best of times. I began to realize the good that runs parallel with good will always outweighs the bad and God makes the difference. HE gives you common sense, joy, peace and HE never lies. Just learning who HE is, is a greater gift than what self-pity offers. Self-pity makes you miserable and grumpy. I was glad HE had taught me that when my Grandmother Lila was getting ready to go to Colorado and taking my twin sisters instead of me.

I was the one who got to go with her as a lost child, and that was good for me. I knew somehow my mother and grandmother were concerned what I would think or do. As I started to feel hurt, the Lord spoke to me and said, "She is their grandmother too." Mother started to explain why and I just said what the Lord said to me, she is their grandmother too.

In time, God would have me look back to this moment as a lesson. I was starting to realize the reason for relationship just as HE and HIS father had a relationship to live this "LIFE." I was not aware that was what was supposed to happen. I had not started reading HIS word. In the beginning was the word and the word was with God and the word became flesh.

When I started reading scripture, for the most part, I did not understand what it meant. I was just like the disciples and I had to keep asking HIM what it means. It was not until later in life while I was in Africa, that I was to learn more that I placed on the shelf for the HOLY SPIRIT to show me the meaning of God's word.

Africa

When I contracted malaria in Africa, God allowed me to be in a coma. It was here that our talk continued. I found myself in the darkest place known to me and I was suspended in air. I found myself crying out "My God, My God, why have you forsaken me?" Then it hit me that was what Jesus was crying out on the cross.

"You did not leave Jesus," I said, "as you have not left me."

"No I did not forsake HIM."

"What is this place?" I asked.

"It is called separation from God."

"Why is it called that?"

"Because there is nothing here that is of ME or who 'I AM'. Do you see any light, anything I created or anything 'I AM?'

"No! So, is that why Jesus and I both cried out and it felt so awful?"

"Yes, you felt no love, no peace, no grace, nothing that 'I AM'. So, it was as if I left you. I brought you here to show you what you choose when you do anything apart from me."

"Lord you can take me to heaven or leave me here on earth but do not leave me here. Now you said I can do nothing apart from YOU so do I have a part in getting out or do you do it all?"

"What have I taught you to break evil's hold?" "Praise you, so I will praise YOU."

Time is different with God, so it seemed like four days of praising HIM, before I was out of that place. I was out of the coma sometime in this process and found my arms tied to the bed rails. That was an equal to the 'Separation from God' experience but in a different way. God already knew my thought of getting out of this trap too. "Father if I get out I may kill someone. So I am asking you for grace and wisdom on what you want me to do." "Win the nurse over."

"Yeah right, and how do I do that when I am so mad and distraught and don't even want to do that? So, I am asking YOU for grace to cope and grace and wisdom on how to do as YOU ask."

It was just two or three days of God giving me wisdom and grace to deliver that to the nurse. By the time I was given permission to fly out Medical Air the nurse could not do enough for me. I can do nothing apart from God and when I choose my own way I have chosen the original sin, "Separation from God." A personal relationship is the only place I can find any kind of help for any situation or crises.

Depart from Me

I can only speak for myself but do others have a personal relationship with HIM? "Lord in your word you say 'Depart from me I never knew you,' so is this the reason you can say this?" "Yes, if someone calls you or knocks at your door and wants to come in and stay and you do not know them, what do you say?" "Go as I do not know you."

In Disobedient

In high school, I was trying to make myself ready to go to college to be a nurse. I took chemistry and the subjects that might help. All the time I was sinning, as I was not asking God anything about this task. I went to Fort Hays State University for nursing school regardless.

The program was strict and harsh. The first semester, they had me taking 18 hours and I was to maintain at least a "B" average. School had always come hard for me because I did not realize that from birth I was going deaf, an inherited problem. Calcium was hardening the bone in my ears causing the bone that went into the nerve to stop sending sound to the nerve.

Needless to say, I did not maintain a "B" average. I dropped out of the nursing program and just concentrated on getting all the required courses out of the way. When time came to choose a field, I had forgotten that the Lord had told me in the fourth grade I would have something to do with art.

I went into Home Economics. I was drawn to that as I liked all of the curriculum as that was everyday living. It was much later in life that I knew from living life with "LIFE" that it was time to go back to school and get my degree in Art.

God just used my general situation to teach me this. Schools had been phasing out Home Economics classes. I could not teach in the district, as my husband, Stan, was the principle of the grade school, therefore I would not be considered for the job.

Art Classes

When Home Economics Teachers were far and few between as the programs were being dropped, it was at that time I was thinking about why I did not get my degree in Art as the Lord had said in fourth grade. I would have something to do with Art. I knew of Marion Walker, who taught some Art classes, because I had her girls in my Home Economics classes in High School.

The high school Art teacher was going into ministry and leaving, so I saw this as God saying it is time. Marian was moving to town. That was convenient for me as I could ride to the classes with her. That is when I started my art training and when I had taken all of her classes I went back to F.H.S.U. as they were considered to have one of the best programs. I went and earned very good grades as I had found out my hearing problem could be corrected with an operation. I went and had both ears operated on and could hear a lot better. From 20 percent in one ear and 10 percent in the other ear to 70 percent and 50 percent. Not perfect, but I would take it.

Living Alone

Since I was living by myself in Hays I had more time to ask HIM things I did not understand. So, I asked HIM to show me how I was saved at five years of age. This is what he showed me. I played "me" in the role-play. HE often has me role-play. I do not know if it was a vision or not.

The first thing I saw myself doing was making an "X" on a piece of paper, as I was entering a contest. It wasn't long and my mother gave me a package and said you won the contest you entered. I opened my ring-sized package and it was a pearl. I was just like any five-year-old and carried it around everywhere.

As time passed and I got older in this role-play, I decided that was not smart anymore and put it away so no one could find my prize and wouldn't lose it. Then one day I started thinking and wondering if it was still there. I started looking for the little box with the pearl. It took me days of looking and finally found it. As I looked at the pearl, I wondered if it was worth anything.

In the role-play I took it to the jewelers. He looked at the pearl and looked. I got nervous and said, "Is there something wrong?" "Not in the way you might think. I am trying to find a way to tell you so you understand what you have here. This pearl is so perfect and flawless that you could buy the whole state of Kansas."

After some thought he said, "I am still not telling the true value of this pearl. You could buy the whole earth and the universe with this pearl." So what do I do if I own everything? No one else will have anything. Then you have to start giving your wealth away, giving "LIFE" away to others.

Then the Lord said this is what happened to you when you accepted me as your savior. "You won the pearl of great price, "ME." That is why I can say in my word, you have everything you have need of at any given time." I asked HIM what I was to do with the pearl, and HE said it is already hidden in your heart in the Garden of Eden where we are now talking. "It is safe and you really do have to give ME away." The HOLY SPIRIT can teach me like no other. She knows me inside out and knows what to say for me to understand.

I wanted to know more than I was beginning to understand more and more that unlike humans HE does not get disgusted with all of my questions. So, I ask HIM why and what HE is meaning when HE said in scripture, "Unless you become as a little child you cannot enter the kingdom of heaven." Again, it has to do with Jesus, as that is the HOLY SPIRIT's job to point to Jesus.

The HOLY SPIRIT explained it to me this way. First Jesus is the word made flesh and so HE obeyed the word and came as a baby. He was then a little child. A little child's most prized possession is the parent or parents. Can you imagine a little child saying, "I do not want you as my parent, I want to do this by myself."

"No! Little children want their parents love, protection and that relationship it provides. I AM that parent and that is how it is to be with you. Unless you become as a little child and want the same things, you cannot enter the kingdom of heaven. Anything other than that you are separated from ME. Did you realize what would happen to a little child on their own. They risk getting beaten up, sexually molested and even sick. Now do they want their parents since these things happened to them like my creation does to ME. You want your own way until it gets you into trouble then you shake your fist at ME!"

"HOLY SPIRIT, why do we have to work out our salvation as you said in your word?"

"There is a lot of wanting of your own way with your own will. Remember when you were young and you set your will not to cry? Have you cried much in your life?"

"No!"

"Can you see the power in that?"

"Yes!"

"One thing you have to work out is how to use that will for MY glory and your good! Everything I allow you to experience is to show you what is still in you that needs worked out or corrected. It is always for MY glory and your good. Experience is your best teacher as long as you have a personal relationship with ME. Otherwise, you will not come to ME for wisdom, direction, common sense, love and teaching. I will always show you Jesus as this whole Life is about HIM."

"Thank you for who you are and being faithful in all things."

More Learning

In a college in some kind of health class, the teacher was talking about syphilis and I had never heard that word so I raised my hand and asked what that was. He got beet red and most of the class turned and looked at me and laughed. When I was alone, I asked the Lord why I got so angry. HE said, "Because righteous anger rose up in you from the HOLY SPIRIT. This is what I AM saying when I tell you that from the heart the mouth speaks. Your mouth spoke, not knowing, not having any experience with sin to learn the hard way what sin causes Syphilis."

On the other hand, out of their hearts a laughter was a knowing. All they did was tell on themselves and the pride that they knew thinking that made them wise. "This is what I mean when I say living always causes pride, diseases and death. Sin must think of themselves more highly than they ought."

Now I knew the meaning of the dream that God let me experience. In the dream, I was walking down the middle of the street and noticed a big farm truck parked, loaded with manure. I was thinking where did it come from. Then I looked down and I was walking in it, ankle deep. I immediately pulled one foot out and was very surprised to find none of it on my shoe or foot.

God said, "What happened in class was an example of MY WORD. You were spotless and wrinkle free. Sin must make fun of you and your ways to justify their sinful ways. Yes of course, but love is the greatest. Some of the class knew what that word meant but did not laugh as that would have classed them with the world and of the world and they did not want it that way. They may not have understood the principle as I AM telling you now but they knew just the same."

Revisiting For a Lesson

Another incident in life that "LIFE" taught me HIS precepts and grace was when I was in the third grade, I spoke about that earlier. My third grade teacher was not very experienced. She used "The Law" as her guide. I was beginning to learn the law that Jesus came to fulfill with HIS blood is what the world lives by. They want others to live by it as long as they are in the position to implement that law.

They that enforce the Law are in danger of misusing the law thinking it does not apply to them. They themselves don't want to be under the Law but want Grace. The best example that I can think of is our government that pass laws for the people but they themselves do exempt themselves from it.

As this teacher used her students to take out her own pain, anger, hurt and heart problems. When I said I did not know something she was asking, she called me a liar. When I misspelled a word, she slapped me in the face. When my brother needed to go to the outhouse, she denied his need. It was the beginning of learning from the HOLY SPIRIT how evil sin works.

If Satan can mess up just one person, say teachers, to think they are no good, then that person will pass their hurt on to someone else. That will help Satan try to hurt others to destroy them. Then evil spreads. I, for many years, wondered how Jesus could suffer so much hurt, pain, ridicule and disgrace at our hands.

When I ask HIM this, He said, "Because I knew the whole of everyone's pain and what they do not know." At the age of 70 when in Africa in a coma from malaria, the Lord took me to a place He called 'Separation from God.'

It was a sum total of nothing. That is why Jesus cried out "My God, My God, why have you forsaken me?" His father was still with HIM it just did not feel that way. When I experienced the same thing, I also cried out the same words. Then I knew how Jesus on the cross could say "Father forgive them they know not what they do."

Again, I am able now to pray for the evilest of the evilest of mankind as they do not have a clue what they do. They do not know what they are choosing. I want them redeemed from this lie and trap of self-will.

Mirror Dream

I cannot forget to tell the dream of the mirror. I dreamed I was in a bedroom and all that was in the dream, at first, was me, looking into the free-standing mirror. As I looked into the mirror it suddenly broke into a thousand pieces and then it was like a light came on and I could see the whole room. It shocked me and I woke up. I said "Lord, what was that all about?"

HE asked me, "What did you see in the mirror," and I said me, "Who did you see when it broke?"

I no longer saw me but the whole room bathed in Light. LIFE said, "When you do not see yourself anymore then you will see me, the Light and the whole of the room."

That seemed clear enough but I found that I still have to live with LIFE to keep working out my salvation to stop seeing me at all.

"When you get self out of the way you will see ME and hear ME. All of the broken glass is all of your hurts, disappointments, sins and un-forgiveness. When the mirror broke it was you giving all of it to ME at MY feet. If you hang on to all of that, you will not see ME. Now do you see what I mean when I say, if you save your life you will lose your LIFE? It is all about you, not ME."

Setting My Free Will

As LIFE took me back to when I was nine at Grandma Mattie's house and I set my will as I saw how crying tended to get others to want to return evil for evil.

My grandmother was crying when her daughter, Ione, came into the house. My grandmother was telling us how her neighbor had hurt her. Aunt Ione was going over to straighten her out.

My grandmother stopped crying immediately and said, "No! It is bad enough that she hurt me but you will not return evil for evil."

That was a powerful lesson for me. I set my will that very minute not to cry. After the Lord reminded me of this, He asked me, if I had ever cried except for in His presence. I said not that I recall, "I reminded you of this to show you how powerful your will is. It is stronger than all of MY power, so I gave you a free will and I will not go against it."

"It matters how you exercise your free will. You can use it for good or evil. Remember each time you do not choose ME, you have chosen separation from ME, the first sin," HE reminded me, "that is death."

Walking Through Life on Earth

I had a dream that I was walking down the middle of the street and saw a grain truck parked on the side of the street full of manure. I wondered where they got so much and then I looked down and realized the whole street was full from gutter to gutter with manure.

I thought they had been cleaning the streets. I was walking in it and pulled my foot out to see that I did not have one drop on my shoes or socks. I woke up and asked the Lord what that meant.

HE said, "Now you know what I mean when I say you are in the world but not of it. What I mean is when you walk with ME in the world you will be spotless and wrinkle free as you will not be of this world.

I asked the HOLY SPIRIT, "Would you show me how being anything apart from you and the importance of separation.

People who have never been in the place called "Separation from You" can't understand unless they have experienced that place.

Numbers

"Do you use and work with numbers?"

"Yes!"

"Then choose one number that will be yours."

"Okay, I choose three as that is YOUR signature for Father, Son, and HOLY SPIRIT."

"Now, with the remaining numbers, will you be able to figure out any kind of math problem correctly?"

"Yes, as I will have all other numbers."

"Do you realize that all other numbers have no three in them? You took it out. Every number takes a three to get into OUR total."

"So I have only one and two to work with?"

"Yes, and if you add that it is three, remember you took that out so what good are those two number to you now? Do you realize that you unknowingly took ME out of everything, with your own wisdom? You can do nothing apart from ME."

"HOLY SPIRIT, You are amazing with YOUR knowledge and wisdom. I thank YOU for who YOU are and that YOU are not haughty, selfish or rude in your teaching. I ask YOU for grace to be just like YOU."

HE then asked me if I recalled the dream of the mirror. "Yes, you had me dream that I was in a room with a free standing mirror and all was dark around the mirror. All I saw was myself in the mirror and suddenly it broke into a thousand pieces. It was lying on the floor, light flooded the room and I could see everything in that room. It startled me and I woke up and asked you the meaning of the dream?

"I explained that as long as you see only you in this world, self, then everything around you is dark. As soon as you let your image be broken, then you see light, LIFE, and there is no darkness around you. This is also MY word when I say you need a broken and contrite heart."

HE continued, "I have made everything that I created to tell about ME, every tree, every blade of grass, every color, every season, everything. Even man was made to tell about who I AM. That is why I can say you will have no excuse from not knowing ME when I return. Yet, some still want to take ME out of the equation and then are angry that I don't care. Even though it was their choice by their free will I gave them."

You took out the number three thinking it was good as it was the number that is MY signature. Then all you had left was one and two. You thought you were a goner without 'LIFE'. Then I asked you to add one and two and you get LIFE again. What did you feel at that moment?"

"I was ecstatic that YOU are still in control of my life because I have chosen YOU, because YOU first chose me."

Forgiveness

I need to tell you about another dream God gave me as I was trying to figure out how I was to forgive someone. I was at a big sports stadium and needed to use the restroom. There were women in all the stalls on both sides of the long room. At the end there were more on a raised cement structure.

No shoes where visible so I knew they were all empty. When I got close enough, I could see that wasn't the case. The stools were all stopped up and there was urine and feces everywhere, it was nasty. I backed out being careful not to get any on me.

I woke up and asked the Lord what HE was telling me. HE said, "What desire do you have in your heart that you have been pondering?" I said, how do we get rid of sin in us? "You do that the same way those stools got rid of waste. If someone dumps on you, you must flush or you get plugged up and no one wants to be near you. You will be disgusting to others like that mess in the bathroom."

"So, people have waste in them and that has to be eliminated?"

"Yes, when you do not come to TRUTH for teaching and understanding, that is when you become plugged. The water in the tank of a toilet is the water of the word that has to be in you. Your tank must be full all the time in order to flush your mind and heart. That's why I say do not let the sun set on your anger. That is similar to not flushing the stool and letting it sit all night."

"How do I, as your child, flush?"

"That is forgiveness and without that you are not clean inside. I created your physical body to eliminate waste the same way. What happens when that gets stopped up?"

"Lord, how can you stand it?"

"I say in MY word that sin is like a rotting decaying cat. I cannot stand it anymore than you."

Go to the Sink

There was another time that I was very frustrated and I needed to talk with HIM and have no one bothering me. I asked HIM to give me the time and place that I would not be bothered. HE said, "Go to the sink." I knew HE meant the kitchen sink and that I should do all of the dishes. I said, "Lord, you know I do not like to do dishes." HE said go to the sink. HE never argues with me.

I went to the sink, filled it with hot, soapy water, and stuck my hands down into the water and we started talking. The kids never bothered me once. When the dishes were done, I was wanting more time with HIM and the joy HE brings and in return HE made doing the dishes a pleasure.

Cabin Dream

I was having trouble comparing myself with others and then falling short in my own eyes. The HOLY SPIRIT began to teach me in a dream. The dream in which I was a small girl sitting in an old burnt out slave cabin with nothing in it.

The Lord had asked me in the dream to stick my finger in a hole on the wall. To me, that seemed pretty hopeless because the cabin had many cracks and they were big enough to look out and see what was going on outside. There was a grain truck full of money and a man giving his money to the people that were gathering. The people receiving the money did not seem really poor. Then I woke up and I asked the Lord about the dream.

HE asked me which one of us was the greatest. I felt as if I was just given the answer as I said we were both equal because we both were obeying you.

The rich man was giving away all his money to come follow you. I, representing the poor of the very poor was obeying you too. I also learned why God said in HIS word not to compare ourselves one with another as if we do we will always fall short. I ask HIM why that was and HE said, "Because I have given you all different gifts and different assignments. I do this so that you will not feel like you are not doing enough because someone else has a different gift that you view as being better."

Law vs. Relationship

The world measures things by the 'Law' and the Law was to show you that it was unattainable. That is why even religions have rules measuring who is good or bad or right or wrong.

"My plan was just simply relationships, with ME first and then to others. Without a relationship with LIFE and LOVE you will not have a very good one with anyone else."

"Lord, how did I know the Truth of the law versus relationships dream?"

"Because you have ME, TRUTH, so you can rightly divide MY Word. We are one in the same. The Word became flesh, that is ME. 'I AM' is one hundred percent the word and everything I do will be inside the guidelines of MY word. I AM the word become flesh so I do everything according to the word. That is how you know MY voice. The world measures everything by the flesh. People in the flesh say me, me, me. The world is selfish, prideful, haughty and all the things Love is not."

"Would you make a box and put on one side all that 'I AM" and on the other side put all the things that are considered evil. No, do not decide for yourself (in the flesh) what the words mean. Look them up in the Greek and Hebrew.

Living Life with LIFE

Tree of Life, Choosing LIFE, Love Stands for Forever

1. Patient
2. Kind (telling others about TRUTH)
3. Never glad about injustice
4. Rejoices whenever TRUTH wins
5. Loyal, no matter what the cost
6. Always believe in HIM
7. Always expect the best of HIM
8. Always stand your ground in defending HIM
9. Gives to the poor, widows and orphans
10. Does not fear
11. A settled mind, knows that God will take care of him and he does not have to demand his own way
12. Protects the simple and childlike
13. Hears God in a personal relationship
14. Trusts the Lord
15. Thankful (the gate to HIS presence)
16. Rejects compromise with evil
17. Obeys God from a relationship with HIM as Jesus did as HIS Father
18. HE is our light and counselor
19. Will prefer obedience to making money
20. Setting our will to YOUR ways of giving us a free will to choose
21. Choose mercy over law
22. Will have common sense to apply the LIFE in everything he does
23. Will not be overcome by evil and do as evil does
24. Keep our eyes on Jesus full of mercy
25. We let the Lord build HIS house
26. Do not pretend to know it all
27. Harmony
28. Become like Him as we trust HIM

Tree of Good and Evil, Choosing Death, Death stands for Evil

1. Jealous
2. Envious
3. Boastful
4. Proud
5. Haughty
6. Selfish
7. Rude
8. Demands its own way
9. Irritable
10. Touchy
11. Holds grudges
12. Notices when others do it wrong
13. Lying
14. Cheating
15. Killing
16. Slander
17. Curses others
18. Causes others to fail
19. Fears
20. Their gods are manmade things like silver and gold
21. Controls others lives
22. Trust men
23. Hate, hate, hate
24. Thinks themselves better than others
25. Becomes like the evil one
26. Not full of kindness except to use it to get their own way

Choosing Not to Be "Of the World"

After time passed, I stopped teaching to start adopting the 'parentless children' God had said I would have something to do within the 6th grade. It was the last year in that school when we were expecting our daughter, as it turned out.

The school district here in our town lost an 8th grade teacher and they came and asked me to take his place. I told them I was going to go with my husband to Fort Sill, as he was finishing basic training, as soon as I could. They said that was all right if I would help them out.

I knew better than to sign a contract and said I would not. I did not want to teach any of the math. The seventh grade teacher said he would take both math classes and I took both science, as I liked and understood that better. We started the second semester and then the principal wanted me to sign a contract.

I do not think I did. When I could go with my husband he said if I left he would see to it I never taught anywhere again.

Talk about anger rising in me. I told him he could just do that as it would be on his conscience and I was honest and straight forward with him from the start. That did not work and his next shot at keeping me there was saying that I owed them money.

I came home and put it to pencil, as his argument was I should pay for the vacation. It turned out he still owed me money for my time. I asked the Lord what had happened. Did he hate women, was he a liar, what?

"He is trying to figure out how to stay in control of the situation and control you. That is a sin." To control another life is sin as God gave you free choice and I do not come against that. Our free will can separate you from ME but unless you ask and seek ME you get to run your own life. I call it being of the world. Trust me to solve this for you. Do not be tricked into being of the world."

We had to come home to get our daughter. I have always felt she was given to us from God. As it turned out, we named her one of Gods names, Nicci, and we did not even know it until years later. It came from Jehovah Nicci, which means someone who is victorious.

The Best of Times and The Worst of Times

During our first years of teaching in Milwaukee, it was the best of times and the worst of times as that is when 'LIFE' taught me the very most.

I had been taught by the Spirit of LIFE how a wolf can come in sheep's clothing. I had to go to a meeting to be acquainted with all the other teachers in the school in which I was teaching. On the way, I turned too soon and ended up in a city within the city.

It was the huge Coors Brewery. It was night and the only light in the place was from the streetlights from the over pass in which I had come. I was calling upon 'LIFE' for wisdom and a sound mind as fear was taking over.

Lord let me remember what I am told to get back on the overpass. I came upon a very little place where two guards were for the night. They looked pretty rough. I rolled down my window just far enough so they could not get a hand in.

I had listened to and remembered the instruction they gave me. That was the first time I had felt fear. I was afraid of being raped. I kept repeating what they said over and over to keep the directions in my mind that fear would not take over completely.

I found my way out and found the school. One male teacher was keen enough to realize I was in a state of fright. He taught on my floor but I just barely knew his name. He sat by me and was ever so kind. He kept encouraging me all through dinner and the meeting. After the meeting, he asked if he could take me home and the next day I could come get the car.

I was thinking the car was probably not safe here all night. Then his wife said she would go with us. He snapped at her to go home and put their boys to bed to relieve the baby sitter. The HOLY SPIRIT warned me that I shouldn't allow him to take me home. If I had listened to the HOLY SPIRIT instead of fear, LIFE would have protected me on the return trip back across the city.

I relaxed in the fact that he knew the city and I would not get lost again. It was not long before I stopped seeing city and only country. I asked in panic what he was doing. The thing I feared came upon me as Job said in scriptures. I have never felt every emotion at the same time.

I felt sorry for this man, hated him, could have killed him and felt compassion and pity for him because he had two small sons. I gave up that night for fear I would kill him. Again, I did not trust LIFE and my fear became a reality. Fear only accomplishes evil.

Then, he took me back to my car and I had to drive home anyway. Now I was more than glad to drive home to be out of this man's presence. I had learned enough this far to know a victim is made a victim repeatedly. Others see it as their fault.

I was begging God for the okay not to tell Stan. I had enough of deceit and fear. From this, I became most aware of how, in God's word, Job failed and got into trouble. Fear blocks faith and obedience to God. In time, LIFE taught me through this experience to trust and rely on the Lord every minute of every day. I eventually told Stan about the experience when it didn't affect me anymore.

The dialog with GOD, LIFE became so open that He became more real to me than anyone around me. It was in these 20 years of living life with "LIFE" that I really began to see who He was. He was so faithful to be there.

Building a Relationship without Satan's Tools

One day I was a basket case inside and I asked the Lord if I would ever overcome this? As we talked, HE taught me that people in pain are the ones who strike out at others or cuss violently when talking. Children in pain kick chairs or call parents rude things and they need LIFE's love, but parents dish back from their own pain.

One day one of my sons wanted to be held and I lifted my arm to demand he clean his room, in demanding, that's law. The Lord said "You cannot lead your children to ME using Satan's tools." Then, HE asked me to list all of Satan's tools as I would know what they were.

I did and we had many discussions as to how he uses them and the damage they do to separate us from HIM. Those 20 years were the best of times and the worst of times.

At the end of that time, LIFE asked me, "If I asked you, would you go through that again?" I did not even hesitate with a loud "Yes!"

"Why," He asked.

"Because I found you and now am seeing who you are and know I can trust you. What I gained does not even compare with the pain and shame."

"What was the worst thing for you?"

"The shame of not catching your leading and the loss of my self-respect," I answered.

"Do you realize you never had any self respect to lose? You lost all that when Adam and Eve sinned. Their self-respect before sin was in ME, LIFE. Adam gave it all up for death, separation from me, selfishness and all the others I had you list previously.

"Lord," I asked, "Is this the way you have become a friend that sticks closer than a brother?"

"Yes, and you can see I did it all. You can do nothing apart from ME. You will learn about LIFE in every wrong choice, in everything that happens to you and some things will not be your doing. It will be because of others choices or mistakes."

The HOLY SPIRIT then recalled a dream I had about being all dressed in clean clothes just walking down the street minding my own business. A mud ball hit me in the side of my face and I was instantly muddy and hurt inside and out.

As I turned to see who threw it, I saw two boys standing by a small mud hole throwing mud balls at each other. One threw a wild throw and it hit me. They hardly realized what had happened.

When I woke up and asked the Lord, He said, "That is the way the world is apart from God, no order, selfish, wanting to be the best or the winner at any cost. It is all a lie. Apart from ME you can be nothing and do nothing as it is all a lie because you have done it apart from LIFE."

"You can be in the world but not of it. In our relationship, I will take you through all things and teach you about Jesus, LIFE in process. That is why I say I get the glory and it will be for your good. I do not worry about mistakes that you make as I am in control for those who love ME."

AFRICA

Home from Israel it was a "Now what, Lord?" It did not take long until I got an email from Homer, the head of the volunteer program in Israel. Claude Meyers, a superintendent of the Mozambique Christian School in Africa received Homer's emails about the volunteers in Israel. In the email, he mentioned that I was a teacher and Claude asked Homer to have me contact him.

They needed a teacher. I sat at my computer, asking, seeking, knocking for days, counting the cost as the Lord asks us to do. Finally, Claude said his wife would be in the states and she can call me and answer any questions that I had.

She called when she came to the states and I asked her what I would be teaching. She said English and I said, I am not qualified to teach English and I do not like or understand English. She tried to convince me that all I had to do was prepare each night. Then, I found out I would be teaching about 18 subjects.

Art alone would have been enough as it takes a lot of preparation. I did not know just how much until I got there and there were no supplies. We had to go to South Africa by car to get them. We had the money, which I was told the school did not. I tried hard to find what I needed, as most Africans all did.

If I did not have to teach English, I would go. When I got there, I didn't know anyone, or any of the cultures and did not have a way to get around. They drove on the left side of the road, had roundabouts and most of the time the street stop lights did not work. We had to drive defensively. The African mind set was we have always walked so pedestrians always had the right of way.

That got many people hurt or killed. One missionary hit and killed a little girl as the child ran out from between cars and into traffic. The mother was an honest person and told the police it was her child's fault. That does not happen as often, most of the time they take the opportunity to make some money.

We had one missionary that hit an African man. He took him to the hospital and paid all the bills. Afterword, the man kept asking him for money. It was a guilt type of bribery. They have so little and the missionaries feel their hurt and misery.

There are four divisions of the department of law enforcing division. Each one does not have authority in any other division. If someone doesn't understand these divisions, they may be taken advantage of and bribed for money.

The couple I lived with knew, so when one day the wrong division stopped us on some technicality and wanted her driver's license. She would not give it to him. She said, "I will go to the police department since I have one day to do so. Besides, you cannot stop any cars as it is not your division job to do so."

He let us go as he did not want us to go to the police department with his name, as they would know he had no authority to stop us.

One missionary was stopped and propositioned. She was smart enough to take down his name off his badge and she turned it over to her husband. He went to the police department and explained the situation. That stopped that.

One night just as three other missionaries and I were finished with supper, automatic guns were firing and all four of us hit the floor in front of the heavy furniture and watched as the trees in our front yard were stripped of their leaves.

That street is noted for such happenings. When the smoke had cleared, the police at the end of the block had captured the gunmen but the driver escaped. They wanted the guard's guns and when they would not hand them over, they started shooting.

In all the firing only one guard without a gun was killed. He was our next door neighbor's guard, many guards do not have guns. That is determined if you are guarding someone in government or high ranking military personnel.

We were informed about some things but we were never prepared for what happened. The superintendent of the school where we taught had a man put his hand in his pocket to steal his cell phone. He would have accomplished it if it were not for his wife walking behind. She saw what was happening and yelled just in time for him to react and grab the man's hand. Evil is not dumb.

James 5:16, "Confess your faults one to another, and pray one for another, that ye may be healed. The effectual fervent prayer of a righteous man availeth much."

This scripture has always perplexed me as to what one does to be in obedience to it. I am to be a doer of the word, the word must become flesh so I can do it. Jesus was the word made flesh and HE is in me. Lord show me or let me see how one is a doer of the word, James 5:16.

"What is confusing to you?" HE asked.

"It is when I am with a girl friend and we are talking about what we have done that was wrong. I feel I am sharing."

"That is confessing your faults with another. Most of the time, neither person seems to have any advice as to how the faults could have been avoided. Unless you come to ME asking, seeking, knocking to find, this is prayer when you come to ME. Prayer is talking with ME. I can then instruct you why, when, where and because of the reason sin has made you stumble. Through this you find out who I AM and become like ME, just as I did on earth I went to Our Father.

A Dream

I was given a dream, where I was at a fair where there were many booths of all kinds. I only had so much money and was looking at what I could get to eat that would be a good buy price wise, and most nutritional. It needed to be a good meal to sustain me. I had finally decided on one booth and after I ordered, I realized I did not have enough money.

I put my hand in my picked and it was full of bills. The money just kept increasing and I woke up in wonder. I asked the Lord of what HE was saying in the dream. He said there will come a time when this will happen. You will be in wonder of how and why you have money when you know you only have a certain amount.

That has come to be Truth from time to time, The first time it happened I did not have money to buy food. I was telling the Lord my problem and was driving into the driveway of my home. I got out of the car and something caught my eye. As I really looked, I realized there was a twenty-dollar bill on the grass.

I went over and picked it up and thanked the Lord for the way He provided. That, in and of itself, was a blessing to see HIM, who He was and another way He provides.

The Spirit of Words

I was asking the Lord why His word seemed dead or lifeless at times. He said, "because words can mean one of three things; lifeless, have life and seeds." I asked HIM to show me how words are like seeds.

He allowed me to role-play and I was talking, and as each word came out of my mouth it was a seed that dropped to the ground, sprouted and began to grow. The Lord showed me how I imprisoned myself with my own words, and how I set myself free with words of LIFE.

The word seeds grow things that set me free by that which is free, Jesus Christ. HE gave us free will and to choose LIFE or death with every word that proceeds out of my mouth. "Out of the heart the mouth speaks." Which shows us what is in our own heart.

"So, HOLY SPIRIT, how do I do this?"

"You see every person as Jesus. Remember when I say whatever you do to the least of these you do unto ME," HE said. "Everything you say is a lie unless you have ME, LIFE and I AM what gives it LIFE. Remember you can do nothing apart from ME and if you choose to do it in the flesh, on your own, you have chosen death which is separation from ME."

Relationships

Lord, you have created everything to tell about Jesus. I know how man and women in relationships create another human life. "How does our relationship create LIFE?"

"In verbal intercourse as we talk, I impart LIFE to you and TRUTH as I AM both. If you do not talk to ME in relationship, there can be no LIFE or TRUTH in you. That is the reason I say you can do nothing apart from ME. In relationship with ME, I impart life to you and then you can say what I say and impart life I gave you to others, just as I said in the written word. I only say what my Father says and I only do what I see MY Father doing. This comes only from relationship."

Going to Sleep

"Father, we have been in conversation for two and a half hours. If I fall asleep should I ask for your grace?"

Remember when you rocked, sang or read to your children, did it upset you when they fell asleep?"

"No, I was filled with joy."

"As I am with you, unless you become as little children you cannot enter the Kingdom. Be a little child and go to sleep."

Gifts

"Remember that I ask you not to compare yourselves with one another as you will always fall short." I said yes. "Remember what my reason is for that?"

"Yes, because you have given all of us different gifts so we would fall short in our own eyes because it would not be our gift."

Dig a Well

I was sitting at the table talking to the Lord and I asked HIM how so many denominations were formed.

"Go look in the well in your front yard."

"Lord, there is no well in my front yard."

"Just because you have not dug it does not mean there cannot be one."

In my mind, I saw myself out in the yard, digging a well. It got so deep that I realized I could not get out. In asking the Lord, HE showed me to place the rest of the dirt I dug out to one side and make a ramp. As soon as I had done that, I climbed out.

There was a man walking down the road and the Lord said, "Ask the man what he sees in the well." The man came over from my asking him what he saw. He said empty space. Another person came and I asked him what he saw and he said air. I said you can't see air, and he said you can breathe it. I asked another and after looking they said a dead bird. That surprised me as I was sure there was no dead bird. I looked and sure enough, a dead bird. I asked another and they said water. Again, I looked and sure enough there was water seeping up.

I had just about gotten to water but it took a little bit of time for it to soak through to the surface. Another man looked and said oil.

"Lord, there is no oil."

"Just because you have not dug deep enough down, does not mean there is no oil. That man sees and knows what you do not see or know."

"Lord, what does this have to do with how denominations get started?"

"The well represents MY world, a well of untapped wisdom and knowledge of who I AM. Every person that came, saw a truth and went and started a denomination on that Truth of who I AM."

"What does the dead bird tell me?"

"Some in the Church are dead in their belief. What all this means is, that in MY word, the oil represents the HOLY SPIRIT and power. Can you not power earthly things with oil? There are different levels of discoveries, you call it layer upon layer, and some say line upon line or precept upon percept. The water is MY word. Without water you cannot live and without MY word the spirit cannot live."

HE continued, "Jesus showed you this by the word becoming flesh. HE was the word in its completeness. HE could do nothing apart from ME or the word. It is like your DNA. What you could not see, like air, is faith. Remember, I have said everything I created tells you about ME in more than one way."

"Thank you, HOLY SPIRIT, for teaching me. What a joy to learn from you."

"You're MY joy that you are teachable and come asking, seeking and finding."

A Dream

When I was in High School I had a dream that a tall white horse came into our yard and had no mane. To get on the horse I would grab the mane and throw myself upon his back. I did not know if this horse was gentle and wanted to know that first. I led the horse around the yard and was surprised that it followed me everywhere I went.

I woke up from the dream, the next night I had the same dream and the horse came into the yard again. Only there was a small tuft of hair at the base of his mane. I grabbed hold of it and still could not get on. So, I led the horse to the fence and got up on the fence and then got on.

We walked around the yard and I woke up. The horse was very gentle. The next night, I had the dream again and the horse had a gold ring around its neck. I grabbed the gold ring and could swing myself up on the horse. The horse took off running and then up into the sky and my feeling was I was safe and could accomplish anything. I woke up.

I never told anyone the dream for years. When I lived in Scandia, Kansas, I went home and there was a woman at the church that was filled with spirit and was ministering. I went and I found myself telling her the dream. She said that is easy as the white horse is the HOLY SPIRIT. That is all she told me. I then began to ask God. HE said, "You have not because you ask not."

I had never asked HIM what He was telling me. It seems the first time the white horse came into the yard was a representation of a part of my life. The second time was another part of my life when the Lord asks me to get to know the HOLY SPIRIT better. I asked HIM to give me grace to do so. The third night told about the last part of my life that I would trust the Lord in all things and the HOLY SPIRIT and I would fly and nothing could harm me. I felt very safe.

Revelations 1:13 talks about Jesus wearing a golden girdle around His chest, just as the horse has a round golden rod around his neck. The rod is God's love and authority.

In studying dreams, I have since learned that 'horse' stands for Time/Work, a specific period of time. Horse's rider is also Nature of time or work: can be happy, confident. Front half of horse in which I seemed to be dealing with in the dream is the first part of time or work, beginning. White stands for pure; without mixture; unblemished; spotless; righteousness; blameless; truth. Gold in scripture means glory or wisdom, TRUTH, something precious, righteousness and glory of God. (Colossians 2:3, 2 Chronicles 16:2, James 2:4)

Dream April 7, 2011

It is always fun to go on a treasure hunt with the HOLY SPIRIT as She makes learning fun. She wanted to teach a lot through this dream. Sometimes She interprets it quickly and sometimes over several hours or days, maybe even months and years. So far, this has been over several months. I did not have some of the information I needed so I waited. I received in the mail, "The Seven Feasts of Israel," and was watching a Jewish man show God's plan from redemption to the end of time through the seven feasts. The end of time to me now is God's finished plan of redemption. When every knee will bow and every tongue will confess that HE is Lord. What a day that will be for all of creation and us.

The Dream background

The dream was framed, similar to a box window cut out to see what was behind the layer on top, like a computer does. It was as if God did not want me to see the whole of this, therefore HE put something over the whole like an obstruction then cut a square like frame so I could see only what HE wanted me to see. What I saw in the framed portion was several colors but the two I saw and the biggest portion of the colors were Orange and Purple. They were in curved line or sweeping design that causes me to think it was moving even though it was stationary.

There were other colors too but these two dominated. I also realized that when the HOLY SPIRIT revealed the dream to me it would put more interpretation on a dream I had in High School. That dream was over 54 to 57 years ago. When God gives you a dream it is eternal as HE is eternal and I never forget the things HE tells me or shows me.

I knew what most of the colors show forth but not Orange or Purple. Orange is made from a combination of two colors Red and Yellow. I asked the Lord if I am to look at it as both Red and Yellow, or just see it as Orange?

It is its own color, just like the trinity. We are all separate individuals but one in nature and being. I knew I was to see Orange as Orange. I had this dream two times back to back. That also will mean something.

Generally, when I have a dream twice it means I need to find an answer as when a dream happens three times it is unchangeable like prophecy. That is not bad it just means I need to know what God is saying to me. The one I had in High School I had three times as a progressive dream and it happened three nights in a row. To finish the interpretation of that dream excited me, and I wanted to know the HOLY SPIRIT interpretation of this one that I might know some more on the one in High School.

The Dream

I saw a square-like framed picture of a design that was mostly Orange and Purple. There were other colors but these two were dominant. It reminded me of God's rainbow with all of the colors. It was a sweeping design and in Art it causes the design to look moving. It seemed in motion. When I had the dream, the second time there was a ticker tape under the edge of the line that created the frame. I was trying to read it but the only word I got was "design."

God always knows what HE is doing and that was the only word He wanted me to get. The rest of all of this was God's word saying it is always moving, never ending or eternal and full of color. As that is what HIS word says. The ticker tape was saying that too. We are always living and moving forward and this is an eternal message.

I felt led to ask a pastor even when I know I needed to get with God as HE is the only one to interpret our dreams. The pastor did the right thing and asked me if I knew what the color Orange meant? I said, no! His interpretation:

Orange is: Hope

Purple is: Vision

Word I saw: Design

"God may be giving you a hope for a vision" HE did right in saying, "maybe." I knew at this point I was not right and that I needed to get with God and do what I knew to do and talk with HIM as this is always HIS plan and purpose for my life with HIM. Everyone is to, as much as possible; interpret our own dreams in the relationship with God.

In My own Strength and Knowledge

Father you created me so you are my true Father. You mirrored who you are by giving us earthly Fathers. I am tired of being agitated so much because I do not understand evil and why we want to turn our backs on You. Do we like our miserable selves that much to hold on to our pride and selfishness?

"When you do things in what knowledge you have and what strength you have it never is enough. It is also out of MY will, which means you no longer have LIFE, STRENGTH, WISDOM, TRUTH, and A WAY. It is just as sinful trying to work your way to heaven, as it is not realizing I work out your salvation within you too. You have nothing to do with your salvation, except be in relationship with ME so in your weakness is MY STRENGTH."

I replied, "I know you have never lied to me, as you cannot. It is not even in your nature as there is no lie in your DNA. That being the word you gave us. I am grateful that I have you to come to for you to show me how things are to be interoperated or interpretable."

Light-V-Darkness

"Father, how should I see myself when I am apart from you and trying to be obedient in the flesh?"

"I AM LIGHT, see yourself trying to walk through your house in the dark by just feeling and not remembering where everything is. All you have to do is turn on a light and see. That is asking ME. When you do not ask of ME, you are saying you don't need ME and you are in darkness instantly."

Pagan or Self-V-Faith with God

"Father how do I see and discern the good from the evil?"

"Look at Elijah and the pagan priest who were calling on their God, which was the Good and Evil tree, apart from ME. Notice how they did everything in the flesh, they cut themselves, yelled and in their own efforts did nothing. Now look at what Elijah did, he trusted ME as he kept making it harder and harder as he knew I wanted to get the glory from this to prove the Pagans did not have any strength on their side, as humans, can never do anything without ME. I loved you so much when I created you I created it this way so you would have to stay in a relationship with ME for me to be your strength. That is what LOVE does."

Admit I am a Sinner

Father, when I asked, you once told me that I am my own worst enemy.

"If you admit that you're a sinner you will also be admitting that you need someone bigger than yourself in order to live LIFE. When you pretend you are not a sinner, even though you say at Church you are, you are lying to yourself and pretending you are better than others. This is trying to work your way to heaven and that is the 'Sin of the World.' You do not want to pay your debt and you do not have to as I paid it for you. Still you are so ashamed that you're a sinner you pretend you are not by pointing the finger at others to make yourself feel better about who you are. The worst injustice is to try to be what you are not. Accept yourself as human and sinner and let MY gift be enough for your sins and the sins of everyone else. Stop blaming, pointing the finger and denying who you really are, let me be your friend that sticks closer than a brother. Let ME be whom I need to be for you, to get you through this world of sin. Stop taking my place and trying to run other people's lives by telling them how to live, that makes ME very unhappy for you to take MY place where others are concerned. That is why I created you to have a family and to be all to everyone that they will ever need. Remember when I said 'I only do what I see MY Father doing and I only say what I hear MY father saying.' That is a relationship and you are to do the same. As you walk and talk with me I show you who I AM, how faithful I AM, that I AM LIFE, I AM TRUTH, I AM LOVE and you will see and do the same. When you saw I never put you down, never scolded you, never shamed you, never called you names, never was impatient with you and always told you the TRUTH as I cannot do otherwise and this is who I AM. You are totally lost without ME because you are already separated from ME. Remember that separation from ME is the Sin. The word of God is MY DNA. I cannot do except what it says and what I ask of you I AM asking that of MYSELF. Follow ME and do as I do with ME."

Freedom

"When you do as you see ME doing and say what you hear ME saying that is freedom. You are free from sin and being a part of ME. I AM the one that sets you free because there is nothing to fail at as you're doing just what you see ME doing and what you hear ME saying. Some of the things you say to others, would you hear ME saying that to anyone? I only scolded the Sadducees and the Pharisees because they were trying to be ME and take MY place and making bigger sons of hell out of themselves than they already were. That is why you must let ME be in control and I AM who I say I AM and can and will do the job to bring others to ME for salvation. Any human cannot and they are only to live the LIFE in ME that others might see ME. Then I will be their LORD and MASTER as I AM with you."

"Lord, this is really freedom. It makes the yoke so light for me to carry and all I have to do is LOVE others the way I see YOU loving me. Thank you for who you are."

Rebellion and Free Will

"Rebellion is when you use your free will to do anything apart from ME. That seems stronger than I AM because I will not go against your choice and at that point you are lost to ME. Your loss is just as great as MINE. At this point, you have chosen 'separation from ME as you say in Africa when I took you to that place called 'separation from God,' when you had malaria, you said you would not wish this on your worst enemy and that is why you cried out, 'My God My God, why have you forsaken me?' Now you have a whole new mind set as to how to pray, whom to pray for and you truly do not want them in this place. That is why, when on the cross, I too could say, 'Father forgive them, they know not what they do.' I AM trying to show you just how much you need ME for all the things I made you to desire. Peace, Love, Truth, Grace, A Way to live, and a Relationship with the Most High God. There is no greater place to dwell and you can do that now and while on earth. The choice is still yours."

"Lord, I will choose you every day with your help."

Depression

"Remember when you were depressed almost every evening at about 5:30 or 6:00?"

"Yes!"

"Remember you would go to our bedroom and block out all light by pulling the shades? You would spend 15 or more minutes in the dark room. Most of the time you would come out refreshed and okay. A few times you would not be any better. You ask ME, why that sometimes it did not work? I told you to look and see what you did or did not do that made the difference. In time you realized the times we talked you came out feeling refreshed. When you did not talk to ME you remained in a depressed state. Then you asked ME why you were depressed at all. I showed you it was your thinking, how you saw things. You saw things as the beginning of the day in the morning and an ending of the day in the evening. I ask you to see all things as beginnings. The beginning of the day, the beginning of the evening, the beginning of Spring, the beginning of Summer as that gives to MY people a looking forward like I AM. This is one key to LIFE, to look forward to a new day, a new season, a new LIFE with ME, a new child, a new job and on it goes. In time, you will have a new home with

ME. Look forward to that. Look forward to talking with Me at all times. Remember you have never been depressed since that TRUTH came to you from our relationship. You only get TRUTH, LIFE, LOVE and Grace by coming to ME, as that is who I AM. You were not even depressed when you had malaria in Africa because we continually talked."

"Thank you Lord for who you are and never changing. What hope YOU give me."

Stumbling

"Father, is there anything about you that can make me stumble?"

"The fact I'm so big, vast and all knowing you tend to limit ME. Who I AM could boggle your mind so you tend to limit ME and give Satan credit for MY creation and not ME. When you try to figure out MY ways and ME with your thinking and reasoning that is sin, separation from ME. Remember the conversation you overheard, 'You can't correct your thinking with your thinking.' Renew your mind by reading MY word and then let the HOLY SPIRIT teach you its meaning. Be like the disciples who continually asked of ME, what is the meaning? I AM also humble and make it simple for you to understand when the HOLY SPIRIT tells you. When you think someone else is wrong do not argue with them. They may be seeing deeper into MY well of TRUTH or knowledge than you are. Just remember you have all you need at any given time, that's ME. ASK of ME and LIVE!"

God's Greatest Desire

"MY greatest desire is to have a personal relationship with MY people." "Why is that?" I asked.

"Without that personal relationship with you I cannot be who I say "I AM." I can't be faithful to you, I cannot keep MY WORD to you and I cannot show you how faithful I can be to you. As we talk, I can show you how I never leave you or forsake you because we always talk so that you know I have spoken TRUTH. I can build your trust, Faith, in ME because I've told you something and you see it come to pass.

I have given you ME and MY WORD to see who; "I AM." Did you ever consider what I told Moses when he asked ME who he was to tell pharaoh who sent him and I said tell him "I AM" has sent you. Take what "I AM" and put it in front of anything I say in MY WORD. I AM FAITHFUL, I AM LOVE, I AM PEACE, I AM GRACE, I AM THE CREATER, and "I AM" that "I AM."

"Then remember what I said to you in Africa when you were weighted down and trying to do MY part and I said to you; This is not about you this is all about ME. Remember how relieved you were?" HE asked.

"Oh, Yes! It was like the pressure was all drained out of me."

"MY YOKE is light because I do it all and you obey and then I help you do that too, in our relationship. Without relationship you are truly lost from ME."

To Be Led by a Little Child

"Remember when you cried out to ME that you were learning and making so many mistakes in that learning that you wondered how you could ever teach your children anything of MY WAYS" HE asked. "I gave you the scripture that you would be led by a little child and unless you became as a little child you would not enter into the kingdom of heaven."

"Yes I remember!"

"Remember how I showed you that?"

"Yes!" I said, "I was going to one of the kids' rooms and they put their arm up as they needed love and to feel safe. I wanted them to go clean their room first and you spoke to me that I could never bring anyone to you with Satan's tools. You wanted me to write down Satan's tools and watch that I did not use them. I was to be like my child and want your love and acceptance above all else. That is how I would enter the Kingdom of Heaven. YOU are the Kingdom of Heaven. It is YOU, not a place that is important. That is what little children see that we don't seem to see any more as adults. I realized that my children were teaching me not I teaching them. But, in learning and then obeying YOU, I am setting an example for them."

"Yes, continue to be faithful to your LOVE."

Tim Tebow

"Remember the Tree of good and evil and the Tree of LIFE? When you're on the tree of LIFE you are bought with a price and given LIFE. That is what Tim Tebow has as he is MINE. Others who come against him are from the Tree of Good and Evil. They work from Satan's tools. So if you are of ME then you will be attacked just as 'I AM' because Satan hates us and he wants MY rule so he can control you as that is who he is. All of my children are working out their salvation and the last thing that goes is control. I do not control you, I lead, and the HOLY SPIRIT teaches and renews your mind. Remember in Africa how hard you fought being in control, when you were sick and you said to ME, "Father I can't will myself into LIFE, so I will you just do it as you did on the CROSS?" I did as you asked because it was within your working out your salvation. **Well done thou good and faithful servant."**

"Father you have never said that to me, why now?"

"When I say this to you in Heaven it will be because you have been an over comer and given up all of yourself to ME. You are no longer in control of anything that you had on the Tree of good and evil. The Tree of good and evil is all about control. When I say this to you in Heaven it will be because you have worked out your salvation with ME in relationship and with MY strength and ME, you have overcome. Now keep learning, obeying and growing in your LOVE for ME, and continue to do so, and 'I AM' will always be needed by you. 'I AM' in you and you're in ME."

Tree of Good and Evil and Tree of LIFE

Lord, I need for the HOLY SPIRIT to teach me about Death and how that works. I am just like your disciples and cannot understand.

"If you are apart from ME, LIFE, then you are dead. That is real death. If you are in ME and I in you, you are LIFE as that is what I AM. In the Old Testament when I AM cleaning house I AM getting rid of the dead ones. They were apart from ME and dead. Do you keep dead things in your house? NO! You search the smell out until you rid yourself of it. That's why I say Death, SIN, is like a dead decaying cat to my nostrils. Those who are apart from ME are dead and decaying and I cannot stand the smell any longer. I use an earthquake, a flood, or plague and do some cleaning. When one of those who are in ME and I in them, they are asleep in ME, when their bodies are put in to the grave. That is in MY word. Even the disciples did not understand what I said, as I hid it."

"I hid MY word because MY plan was for you to come to Me, just like MY disciples did and ask of ME the meaning. You can do nothing apart from ME, when you choose death then you no longer wanted LIFE, "ME," and are apart from ME. There is only one way to be alive and that is in ME. You can come to ME and ask again and that is asking ME for LIFE. You need air to breathe. Remember when I created Adam he was just a block of flesh and bones with no LIFE, until I breathed into his nostrils. That was the breath of LIFE. I took Eve out of Adam so she was taken out of one that was already alive in ME. Then he and Eve disobeyed and chose death, apart from ME."

"That is why when your loved ones fall asleep in ME and are put into the ground it is the separation from them you miss. The personal relationship you no longer have. It is the same with ME. Remember you were created in MY image and that is part of MY image. All your problems are created because Adam and Eve brought separation into this world. Only the ones that have chosen to be apart from ME are dead. I almost killed Moses because he was apart from ME as he did not circumcise his son. His wife took control and circumcised their son and saved Moses' life. Come and be part of ME and LIVE by asking, seeking, knocking and finding."

January 12, 2012 Dream

I dreamed I was in a many room building in my own room and several people came in and created a lot of confusion. One was using the telephone several times and I said don't make long distance calls on my phone.

He said, I'm not getting a hold of anyone anyway so it will not cost you anything. I asked them all to leave. They did and I noticed it was too dark so I went over and turned on the light and nothing happened. Then I looked up to the ceiling light, all three bulbs were gone.

I looked at the lamp stand light and all the bulbs were gone. I knew what the group had been doing while one of them distracted me, taking the bulbs. I went down the hall and every light bulb was gone. I woke up and asked the Lord what HE was saying.

"Just letting you know that others will be stealing your light as you are the light of the world."

"Lord," I asked, "What does the light bulb represent and what meaning should I take from it?"

"Drought in the SPIRIT is no word, no relationship with the light, ME gone."

"Lord, how will evil steal our light? We have a free will so we will have to choose I would think, but in the dream, they just took it. Show me how that looks. What will be used to distract me that I am missing, what is happening?"

"The key is a relationship with ME. Evil can steal, maim and kill the body but it cannot steal ME, LIGHT. Unless you are deceived into thinking, you no longer have ME. You prove you still have ME by coming and asking, seeking, knocking and find ME and MY wisdom.

Dream February 11, 2012

A woman was requesting that I send her a drawing that I have done. I asked her when she wanted me to send it, and she said this evening! I could hardly get one ready in that short of time, but she put a huge sheet of paper on the wall and gave me some chalk. I wanted to fill up that huge blank piece of paper so fast, so I started drawing trees like a forest. I was thinking that's really not as good as I would like, so I covered it up and I started a huge tree in the foreground.

While I was working, I did not realize the woman was also drawing. When I stopped and stepped back to view it, I was amazed at what was happening. She had drawn a dead tree trunk. The trunk had a hole in it and would be a great focal point. I had commented on the hole and she thought I did not like it so she covered it up with one stroke of the chalk and then it looked like a board.

I was very disappointed. I wish she had asked me what I was thinking. Now what to do, I was going to use the dead tree with the natural hole and it would be the focal point of the whole picture. When I woke up, I asked the Lord what LIGHT HE could give me about the dream.

"It is about you," HE said, "You think you make a mistake and instead of asking ME, you do something apart from ME. You were the other lady. The part you were in the Dream is ME. Can you see the problems you set up by not asking of ME, MY thoughts, and MY intents?"

Deception, Choosing, Blame

"Remember the hardest thing for humans to do is to be Truthful with themselves. It is your Sin Nature, that wants to sin. This process is to show you the Sin Nature that is in you. I showed you that at age nine so you knew you needed to choose. You did, you chose ME. I say in MY WORD 'choose this day who you will serve. You will hate ME and love Sin or you will hate Sin and love ME, you cannot serve two masters.' You will find out, just as Paul did, that what you do not want to do you do and what you want to do you cannot seem to do. You will work at working out your salvation every single day until I call you home. Your greatest help in time of trouble is the HOLY SPIRIT that I sent you. Talk to the HOLY SPIRIT all the time. I say pray continually and this is what I want for you. Talk to the HOLY SPIRIT continually about all things."

Disobedience

"You heard MY voice but you let your fear override your obedience and you chose to do it your way, thinking it was a better way and you would be saving yourself from what you 'feared' but what you got was what you feared. That is why I say fear not."

HE continued, "I have created everything in this world to show you MY ways. Remember the dream I gave you about the toilet stool, how it is an example of getting rid of waste that represents sin. Your body is made to get rid of waste. I have made that to show you the importance of getting rid of it, as it will kill you. Sin kills too. What happens in the physical world shows you what happens in the spiritual world. It is to help you see, to understand. You will have no reason to say to ME when I come back, you did not know. If you try to keep your body from functions as I created it you are telling ME you want to hang on to unnatural ways that are not MINE. It is important that I made you to have accidents to get rid of waste, so you can learn by those accidents. In the spiritual you forgive, in the natural you flush the toilet. Your obedience is the crowning of glory. That is MY goal on earth to obey MY FATHER. It is to be your goal on earth to obey in the same way. There is no greater way of LIFE than obedience. It is a virtue; it is a safe place in times of trouble. It is what makes you without spot or wrinkle. Your obedience to ME, MY WAYS, this is what set you free from Sin and physical Sin, if that is what you want to call it. This does not mean you become others mats to wipe their feet on. I AM your biggest blessings because I AM your FAITH, I AM your HEALING, I AM your FORGIVENESS, I AM that I AM.

Wise and Foolish Virgins

"Lord, I still do not understand the five foolish virgins and the five wise. Please help me know what you are saying."

"Have you ever had a child of mine say to you that they knew the main basic TRUTHS of my word and that was enough? Well that is a foolish virgin, as they don't think they need more oil to keep their lamp burning. "I AM" the LIGHT of the world but the HOLY SPIRIT was with ME on earth being MY oil to keep MY lamp burning. Now you have ME, LIGHT, within you but you need to replenish your oil supply constantly to keep your lamp burning. What you have done by asking of ME, so the HOLY SPIRIT could teach you, is keeping oil in your lamp. It builds your faith, that is ME in you. The relationship with TRUTH, the HOLY SPIRIT and ME is necessary. WE are all TRUTH."

"See MY word as your house in you," HE continued, "and see the lights in your house as ME. See the HOLY SPIRIT as the electricity but if you do not turn on a switch to bring us all together, you have nothing. The switch is your asking, seeking, knocking and finding us all as one. Now that all is clear in your house, you can see things clear in THE LIGHT, as TRUTH. That is the HOLY SPIRIT and ME. This process if filling your lamp, The HOLY SPIRIT and I are one. We do not do anything apart from each other and that is the same with the Father. You cannot get to the Father except by ME, as We are one. The same as you are to come one with us. That is keeping your lamp filled. You are created in MY image so you too can create from what I have created. You can find the principle and create to see who I AM. Light, electricity, power and energy are MY plan that you see ME at every turn. That is why I can say you will have no excuse for not knowing ME. Only when you want to be like ME in the wrong manner, will you try to rule over MY creation, MY plan and ME. I gave all my created mankind a free will. When you try to control anyone else, you are in Sin. Satan is always in Sin as he tries to control others. My throne was MINE from the beginning and it will always be MINE. So choose this day, whom you will follow.

Fresh and New Every Morning

The Lord and I were talking about the volunteer job with CASA I felt HE wanted me to do. How I should be in this job in HIS eyes. The HOLY SPIRIT put me in a role-play. I had a woman that I was assigned to see. The HOLY SPIRIT took over in me and I listened as the Spirit visited with the woman so I could learn.

The love that I felt from the HOLY SPIRIT's words were healing. I knew the woman was also knowing and experiencing that same love. Then scripture came to me about love being the greatest of all and that is why GOD is LOVE. I found myself then realizing why the morning is fresh and new every morning as it is because of our relationship with HIM.

Two-Edge Sword

I was trying to cut frozen bread with every knife I had and still had no luck getting it to cut. Then, I thought about needing a two –edge sword. GOD reminded me of my electric knife. As I took it out a new concept came, and the Lord asked me if this could not be a two-edge sword. I said I guess it is although I never considered it as such.

"Why," he asked.

"Because my mind did not consider it because the knife is something I do not use often."

"Always keep an open mind as the man who invented this knife did, it shows MY word."

Strength

"Father, show me how to see your strength."

"How do you see strength? As the Romans did, Might makes right. Remember when I showed you ME on the cross and I ask you what takes the most strength. Dying for ME or living for ME?"

"Lord, living for YOU, myself, takes a lot of strength, dying definitely took more strength."

"Yes, you are right," HE said, "and that is why many do not follow ME as evil does not have any rules and evil can do whatever it wants. It can lie, it can steal, it can kill and destroy, it can have pride it can gossip, it can pit one person against another, it can do whatever it wants. I AM not conveyed, and they are choosing separation from ME. That equates to they are choosing Death. I am LIFE and one has to choose ME to have LIFE and live more abundantly."

A Good Wife is MY Gift to Man

"Father, why is a wife your gift to men?"

"First, creating must show who I AM. To do this, you must look up on the trinity. You have a Father, a Son and the HOLY SPIRIT, which is female gender, in this circumstance. She represents the wife as my gift to men. She was with me on earth and my gift to guide me and strengthen me. She is your teacher. Who on earth teaches you for the most part, your mother? Now look at another one of MY creations. Look at the mother bear, hippopotamus, the lion or any other of the animal kingdoms. You will see it is the mother who guards her young. She teaches them, protects them and never leaves them. Unless they are born with an instinct to stay in the den when the mother goes to get food to feed them. The HOLY SPIRIT is very vital to your safety, teaching and getting food. In most cultures, it is the women who raise the food, can it, and prepare it. Remember in Africa you wondered what the men did to provide. It is getting better as they find ME and are renewing their minds. An evil husband can destroy a 'good wife.' That is why I ask you not to marry someone that is not already bound to ME."

"Even then, you must ask and inquire of ME, I AM the only one that knows the intent of the heart. Remember what you learned in one of your jobs. A person can hold who they really are from you, for nine months, then, they will have to be who they really are and you will see. Remember the man you were engaged to and in time, you saw who he really was. Men seem to think if they are the head of the house that means they can do whatever they want to do and if they are evil on top of that, you are in for big trouble. I AM the head of the Church, MY BRIDE, but I always let you choose. I do, as I want all my children to know and do. That is why every child of MINE needs a relationship with ME. They cannot learn from me without a personal relationship with ME. To hear and then speak what I say and see ME do and then do what they see ME doing. That is the only way. You are all one in ME. No one is above the other. That only creates problems. You are both, man and woman, to agree if you are to walk together. Remember I say the man or the wife can divorce if the unsaved one wants it. You can't walk with ME unless you agree with ME the TRUTH. Walk and talk with ME then you will know the TRUTH and it will set you free."

To Rule and Reign

"Lord, why is it so important that evil controls our lives and tells us what to do and tries to deceive us?"

"Remember my word," HE said, "where I say in the Church if a King comes in or anyone else, all are equal in ME. Slave, free, king, male, female, rich or poor, are all the same in ME. This is the biggest reason others are trying to eliminate the Jews and Christians. They are free. Without ME, you cannot be free. They know they need to eliminate the Jews and Christians just as Hitler tried to do. Satan will try to mock ME in this way and he will lose. Anyone who tries to mock ME will lose."

"Lord, you are prefect to all and in all. Thank you for your plan to save us from ourselves. We truly are our own worst enemies. I can see that Satan really wants to help us choose evil instead of YOU. It is unreal to think that I would hate my own parents here on earth, or put it another way to hate YOU that created me for yourself as you are my Father in heaven."

TRUTH v. Lie

HOLY SPIRIT teaches me about Truth verses Lie because I ask HIM.

"TRUTH is a person and Lie is a person. Jesus Christ is the person that is the TRUTH. A lie is Satan and was so because he chose that when he said 'I shall be like the most high God.' The only way any person can be TRUTH is by humbling themselves and repenting as they are born a lie and are on the tree of Good and evil. All people were put there because of Adam and Eve's sin that Satan did. I will be like the most High God, also called separations from God. Jesus is the tree of LIFE as HE is LIFE. To accept or choose Jesus, LIFE, that person is made LIFE, in HIM. Every person who chooses ME is of the Family with MY FATHER, Jesus, and ME, The HOLY SPIRIT."

"From the day you are conceived," HE continues, "you are on the tree of good and evil. It is your choice to change trees by the free will I gave you. To never change your mind and stay on that tree of good and evil will be your choice to be forever separated from ME. Just because you can do good from that tree is always with the wrong intent. I know the intent of everyone's heart and if you are in a relationship with ME, TRUTH and LIFE, you will not make as many wrong choices and then when you humble yourself and repent you are back on the tree of LIFE, forgiven. A person has to continually choose ME every minute, hour and day to keep on that straight and narrow. It is that way, as you have to keep in relationship with me in order to stay on that straight and narrow road without falling off."

Jesus is the only person that did that and HE did it for all who want the same as HE died for all people if they chose HIS way. The Ten Commandments were a way of telling you no one could keep them but Christ. So, your salvation and Heaven is HIS work not yours. Just stay in relationship with HIM that HE can be your strength in your weakness.

"When a person comes to you doing good, saying and doing all the right things this is what I call a wolf in Sheep's clothing. He is doing well for the wrong reasons. In time, their hearts desire will become evident to all. That is what I call everything done in the dark will come to light. Remember you learned that about trusting fear instead of ME and you were raped. This man's evil heart came to light and you saw your mistake. As long as you learn to discern as in experience and come to ME you are always forgiven even before you ask."

"You see I love you so much and want a relationship with you, as the reason I created man in the first place," HE said. All mankind is loved by ME and when Adam and Eve sinned and wanted to be separate from ME they choose sin. You need ME to know what spirit is trying to work in you or another person at any given time as all people are working out their salvation or still on the tree of Good and evil, and don't even want ME. This is why many still on the tree of Good and evil will use the excuse that the people on the tree of LIFE, at times do not look any better than the ones still on the tree of Good and evil. The people on the tree of LIFE are sincerely trying, and I say in scripture, as long as you are trying you are okay with ME. The tree of Good and evil, is not even trying, and if they are doing good to earn their way to Heaven that is still apart from ME and evil. That is what evil is, apart from ME. The people on the Tree of LIFE are still working out their salvation, allowing ME to restore them to MY likeness, that takes time."

"HOLY SPIRIT," I asked, "show me how the light YOU created reflects who YOU are, TRUE LIGHT for TRUE LIGHT."

"I AM pure uncreated light and the light you have on earth from the moon and the sun, electricity, and candles or batteries, are created by you from MY principles that I created. Anything created is sill all from ME to attests to ME and who I AM. Any light on earth gives you the ability to see and dissipates the darkness. There is no darkness except when the LIGHT is not there. The Church is to be MY LIGHT on earth as I AM in you. When the world is in a mess or darkness then the Church is hiding its LIGHT. You can see how much good the LIGHT that I created for you and how you could not do without it. Nothing would grow, the earth would become too cold to live, the darkness would overwhelm you and you would die. The same with not coming to the true pure uncreated LIGHT, ME, you will not grow in MY likeness. To see how much you need the created light, you are to see just how much more you need ME, the pure uncreated LIGHT. When MY light shines in your soul and spirit, no darkness can stay. Then you are no longer on the tree of Good and evil, but on the tree of LIFE where the LIGHT shines and things begin to grow and live with LIFE. Ever hear of the saying 'dead man walking?' that is a good way to describe those still on the tree of Good and evil."

Tabernacle / Temple

"Lord, what are you showing us through the Tabernacle? Everything you created tells about you."

"The Tabernacle was a moving Tabernacle. To show you that I AM always moving, I AM always doing, I AM always protecting, teaching, guiding, forgiving, loving, caring, healing and being. Then a Temple was built that was temporary in Jerusalem to show that I will rule from there for the 1000 years after MY coming the second time. Now the temple is in you as it was always intended. It seals you for all eternity, to keep you in TRUTH, LOVE and LIFE. This is why I can say whatever you do unto the least of these my brethren you do unto ME. I AM in you and someone does evil unto you, they do it unto ME. You are to ask ME to bless them. If you do not, I cannot correct them. To bless someone is to be corrected. Remember I said, if I do not correct you I do not love you. This is a great blessing to be corrected so you know I love you.

Tree of Life

"LORD, how does your tree of LIFE bear fruit?"

"When you come to ME in repentance you are then on the Tree of LIFE, ME. Only now can you bear good fruit. You still have your salvation to work out and you do that by bringing everything to ME. All your disappointments, hurts, anger, un-forgiveness, questions, and MY Word, that the HOLY SPIRIT can teach you its TRUTH. You cannot interpret it on your own, in the flesh, as that is sin. Remember we have talked about the first sin, separation for ME. MY people keep doing the first sin. You choose the place of separation with ME when you do anything apart from ME. You can only bear fruit when you're in relationship with ME. That is why I say, pray continually. That means I AM your partner and friend all the time. If you learn anything, learn this one thing, it is all about relationship with ME. I AM the TREE OF LIFE and fruit will not grow without ME. You abiding in ME, will bear fruit without effort. Because of who you are in ME you will say only what I have said and do only what I have done. That is bearing fruit. The Sadducees and the Pharisees are an example. I said you have to obey them but do not do as they do because they are not one with ME in a relationship. That is why they did not know ME. They cannot know ME because I speak the TRUTH and they did not know ME. They cannot know ME because I speak the TRUTH and they did not recognize the TRUTH. I said they were not of ME."

Deception

"Deception is when you make yourselves God or try to take MY place," HE explained. "That is what Satan did in the very beginning. When you try to live in relationship with yourself, you are doing the same thing Satan did. It is called being selfish, trying to work your way to heaven without ME. You will be unforgiving, arrogant, a know-it-all, thinking yourself wise and you are not. You will feel in control but you are out of control. You will be self centered, haughty, rude, living a lie. There will be no TRUTH in you as I AM TRUTH. If you do not think you need or want ME you are a lie. This makes you selfish as you cannot share yourself with anyone."

Taught by Example

"As you work out your salvation, ME in you and you in ME you will see how I treat you an how I act with you so that by experience, with living LIFE with LIFE, you will become like ME. That is what our relationship is all about. That is why where there are two or three gathered in my name I AM there also. If each of the two of you are walking in relationship with ME and you get together then I AM there as I AM in you. You are having church. I never leave you or forsake you, so sometimes it is just two of us, you and ME. So MY word is true, where there are two or three I AM in the midst of you. Just like the Father, Son and HOLY SPIRIT. WE are three and we are one, in each other too. That makes us one. I AM the friend that sticks closer than a brother, you and I have become one just like the Father, HOLY SPIRIT and I are one. Remember what your earthly Father and Mother taught you by what they said and what they did? Tell about what you learned from just having a relationship with them. Your earthly Father and Mother are to show you, also, who I AM, as they too, should have learned who I AM and be doing as I do as they are an example to you and your brothers and sisters."

Where Much is Given Much is Required

Lord, it seems to me that YOU always ask us to do the harder things in this world. We have all this sin from birth and then YOU find us and bring us unto yourself. YOU start renewing us to be with YOU in relationship, to make us into YOUR image again. Satan seems to have no rules and he can destroy and kill and everything in-between. Why is that?

"I AM the bigger person, God and being. Remember in MY word I say where much is given much is required? I AM that word so I will do that too. You and I can, because you have ME. Remember the other scripture that I say you can do all things through ME who strengthens you."

Thank you Lord, it always makes me feel safe and loved when YOU also do what YOU ask me to do. Thank YOU for who YOU are and that YOU are in control of the LIFE YOU gave me.

I want to say what the Lord told me. When I was 28, I found myself falling on my face in my living room and crying out to God that I hated this world and sin and myself a sinner. HE said, "Call me Lord." I could not do it and I asked HIM why? HE said that you can only call ME Lord with the HOLY SPIRIT and HER drawing you to that.

I asked HIM to allow that to take place. Then I asked HIM what I was to do, if anything. HE said I want you to study MY WORD and look up things in Greek and Hebrew. I asked HIM where HE wanted me to start. HE told me to start where HE did, in the beginning. So, I did and I read about the creation and it was good. Each day was creating and it was good. By the time I got to the last day and it was good, I asked the Lord, I was now calling HIM Lord, why do you keep calling everything good?

HE said, "Because everything I created shows you ME. I created everything to tell you who I AM." Then HE told me about the man, woman and child from that relationship. I ask HIM how that shows HIM? He said, "I AM Father, the Son Jesus, and the HOLY SPIRIT, who is a female gender in this scenario."

What HE created here for us, a family of man, woman and child or children is to show who HE is. That is why homosexuality is all about destroying God's image, it is an abomination to HIM. HE explained that HE is LIFE and when HE speaks LIFE into us in our relationship with HIM and then we speak that life into another. Then, they accept Jesus the son's sacrifice for them, they are also a child of the Lord, so we have created new life. That happens when we accept Jesus as our only gate to heaven.

In Revelation, it tells us that in the end of time, it will be as Sodom and Gomorrah. So, it seems we are at that point with homosexuality. When we have done all we know to stand, then we stand.

Taking Offense

"Lord, how can I keep from taking offense or being hurt by what others say?"

"Remember what I say, out of the heart the mouth speaks. When a person speaks hurtful words or calls others names or points a finger, that comes from their own heart. Only I know the intent of people's hearts. Anything that happens to you or you experience evil or good, I can teach you TRUTH from MY word. When I do this, it is called in Scripture, working things out for MY glory and your good for those who love ME. Experience is your best teacher. If you come to ME asking, seeking and knocking to find the TRUTH, you always do, because you find ME."

The best example of this is when HE asked me to read Job. I did, and when I was done, I asked HIM if I gained from it what HE wanted. HE answered, "Read Job." I read it a second time, I began to see I have not seen the TRUTH of the three friends that came accusing Job. Again, HE said, "Read Job." I read it a third time and I suddenly understood! Three friends were going to come to me and do the same as Job's friends did to him.

It was just a few days, and three of my friends knocked on my door and asked to come in. As we sat at my table and talked for a few minutes, one of them said that they all felt that I was possessed and they thought that I needed to be "de-possessed." After they left, I asked the Lord if it were true that I was possessed, and HE said, "Yes, with ME." Then I asked HIM what I was to do about the situation. HE said I was to go to the de-possess session. I asked HIM why, and HE said, "Because, you are to be like ME. I was not guilty either, but if I had not died for your sins you would still be in them. That is what I want from you, go and I will not leave you or forsake you. Then I will ask you as I did Job, to pray for them.

As the pastor and his wife and one of those friends that came to my house were praying for me, the pastor's wife became disgusted and started to shake me saying to me, you need to help us. My thought was, I have nothing to do with this. This is between you and God. When it was all said and done and I left the house, one of those friends said to me, I'm glad to have our sister back. I asked the Lord what if I had not gone.

He said, "Then they would have always thought that you were possessed. Look into My word and see if I ever accused anyone of anything. You will find as you read and look that I always use MY own word because I AM the word made flesh. It is like MY DNA and can do nothing apart from it. I always went asking, seeking, knocking to find. Even when others came to ME for healing or any other problem, I always asked them what do you want of ME? To bear others' sins and burdens is not an easy thing to do. You could not have done this without ME as I also had MY Father and the HOLY SPIRIT to help ME just as you do now."

Satan Comes to Kill and Destroy

"Remember when you were a sixth grader," HE asked, "and I imparted you to what was in your future. You drew upon your knowledge at this point of what you knew. Because you were doing it apart from ME, you were sinning. The only thing you knew about parentless children, were orphanages in other countries. So, you began to plan on being a missionary. There is no place in your life, even if you become 1000 years old, that you will ever know enough when I tell you something. This keeps you close to ME because you will always need ME. Satan cannot kill and destroy, as long as you are in close relationship with ME. The very instant that you decide to go your own way you are in sin. In a relationship with ME is the key to survival in this world from sinning."

Making the Diffrence

HOLY SPIRIT, show me another way that shows us about our relationship with the three in one.

"You need to look at Saul and how he had the word and was taught all his life. He went around trying to kill and destroy those who believed in Jesus. That is an example of reading the word without meeting or having a personal relationship with US. Then Saul met Jesus, and it changed his name from Saul to Paul, it changed his whole life. He had met the word made flesh and received LIFE. Now you have seen what Paul was able to do with a relationship with US. Would you rather be like Saul or Paul?"

"The difference," HE continued, "was the relationship with Jesus who is LIFE, TRUTH, LOVE, I AM and THE WAY. All of this is not in and of itself, it is a person. It is US the three in one. LOVE is a person, TRUTH is a person, THE WAY is a person, THE I AM is a person, and THE TRUTH is a person. There is no other LOVE, LIFE, TRUTH and THE WAY. If you do not have HIM you have none of what I have just shown you. To be like Saul is to be on the Tree of Good and evil. To be like Paul is to have met Jesus, to be on the tree of LIFE and then ME to renew your mind and then you can get to the Father. Remember the word says you can only get to the Father by the way of the Son.

LIFE and THE WORD

Help me understand your thinking on who you are and what the WORD is.

"In the beginning was the Word, it was written down. The Word was with God, it was with ME, Jesus, and the Word became FLESH. Not until the written word puts ME, LIFE as LIFE giving to the WORD will it be alive to you. When I walked and talked with Adam and Eve every evening in the garden, it was not enough for them to not sin, they needed to get to know who I was and Satan found his chance to get to Eve before she walked with ME to trust ME. Sin is death. They chose to be apart from ME, LIFE. Notice how the disciples had to ask of ME when I said anything, WORD. It was "I AM," LIFE that brings the written Word to LIFE. Sin, apart from ME, is Death or already dead. The disciples also had to walk and talk with ME long enough to trust ME. That is why I, Jesus came into the world to witness to the TRUTH. Can you have a coin without two sides? The WORD is one side of ME and LIFE is the other side of ME. One does not work without the other. I could put it another way and say, with your DNA, you cannot be anything different than what you are. So think of the WORD as MY DNA and without it, DNA, the WORD, I can do nothing or it can do nothing with the breath of LIFE, ME. It takes both the WORD and ME to be alive."

"Sin is death when you chose to be apart from ME, LIFE," HE continued, "then you are dead. Just one half of you are walking around dead, because you do not have what makes you alive. That will always be ME. When Adam and Eve chose evil, being apart from ME, they chose death, sin, evil, lies, being apart from ME. You, MY creations tried, in your own efforts of deadness, to clothe yourself and hide from ME. You are thinking with your thinking now, not my thinking of TRUTH. The first thing they did was hide and I knew they had sinned. They could not stand MY LIGHT. No one needs to hide when walking with ME in TRUTH. Those who are dead want and do kill those who walk in TRUTH, as they cannot stand to see the TRUTH. They cannot stand to see the LIGHT in their own deadness. So, it is like Satan is seeing ME in you and can't stand the LIGHT. Think of it this way, if you were in a dark cave for some time and came out to the sunlight, you would not be able to see. It is the same way when you walk as a dead man, apart from ME. Even when you have ME with you and in you, we talk continually just as I say in MY WORD. PRAY continually. Praying is coming to ME for WISDOM, and TRUTH, as I AM the only place you can get it. There is no other TRUTH or LIFE but ME. Prayer is not telling ME MY business or how to do MY plan. You need to come asking, seeking, knocking to find wisdom."

"Remember the word says Ask, Seek, Knock and Find," HE said. "You are to find ME, TRUTH for answers, wisdom, direction and what your part is in any moment of any day or time. When you think someone has said something deceptive from where you are walking with ME. Go to them and ask, seek, knock to find what they mean and DO NOT go accusing. The reason you are drawing upon the things you know of and the experiences you have had and that is never enough for you to decide. Come to ME first then go for understanding, as you do not know the heart the way I do. I planned it that way so you have to come to ME, TRUTH, No one's mind is renewed completely and will not be until you see ME face to face. Then you will be like ME. That is sin and you are trying to take MY place as Satan did. When you take MY place as the MOST HIGH GOD you are just like Satan. He wanted to be like the MOST HIGH GOD. Now he is apart from ME and in darkness and cannot find his own way or a way for you. No one is to take MY place, as that is why I created you to have a relationship with you. This is the one thing that will anger ME more than anything for any human to take MY place in our relationship. That is like another person taking our spouses place of your husband or wife. That is why that is sin as it does not tell in TRUTH who I AM."

"Remember," HE continued, "you asked ME who was your worst enemy and I said, you. You have a free will and to operate in that free will, without ME, makes you your own worst enemy. The free will is a gift from ME and you have to learn how to use it. You can either use it for Good or evil. You can only use it for Good with ME. Even a government of any country is not to take my place in your lives as that is them taking MY place. They are treading on dangerous ground. When you have so much power and wealth, you are sealing your own fate. Power corrupts, complete power and the love of money corrupts completely. That is why I say it is easier for a camel to go through the eye of a needle then it is for a rich man to enter the kingdom of heaven. MY word is TRUTH but it takes ME to tell you it's meaning. That is so you will keep seeking me, TRUTH, as you are lost without ME. I AM obeying MY own word and making learning fun. If I just come accusing you and say, you are in sin, that would not be very exciting and you would not learn anything, or learn to trust ME. Every person I created has a free will and wants a relationship with someone that is not bossy or pointing the finger. Others put you down because they do not see as you see. That gets really binding into a box and they do not want you to get out as they can keep you under their control. That is not MY plan for anyone. The WORD must become flesh for you by being in a relationship with LIFE, ME."

"Come and fellowship with ME," HE said, "TRUTH and LIFE, and you will have all of that. The Word and I are one but you only have the Word and through it you can find ME and then and only then are you whole. I died to give you your place back that Adam and Even lost for all of creation. If you had been Adam and Eve you would have sinned too. My word is hidden from those who do not want ME except to do as Satan did, to rule over others. Satan does know the word but he does not have ME any longer. That is the difference, he has death and a lie, and if you have ME, you have LIFE and TRUTH and can come to me for discernment and wisdom. I AM the only one that can tell you the meaning. For the most part the world is run by Satan's rules of greed, hate, blame, killing, destroying, jealousy, shaming others, gossip, lies, control, cheating and these are all lies. It does not come from the TRUTH, ME. You cannot understand ME without the HOLY SPIRIT and the HOLY SPIRIT is the one who draws you to ME when you hear MY WORD. Ask of ME and find TRUTH. Choose this day, whom you will follow. That means every single day, you choose.

CPSIA information can be obtained at www.ICGtesting.com
Printed in the USA
LVOW120959020812

292506LV00002B/2/P